BREAKING THROUGH

THE GENDER BARRIER

By: Dani'El Garvin

DEDICATION

I dedicate this book to one who knows how to
break through the gender barrier with her love
and acceptance:
To my great friend Brice Milliron

TABLE OF CONTENTS
CHAPTER.....TITLE.....PAGE

INTRODUCTION

Statements like, "I'll never understand a woman," or, "He's just living in a man's world," show how vast the gender gap really is today. Can we really understand the other's culture and the essence of their gender in our binary climate? We spend so much time and effort trying to prove our masculinity or femininity, that we rarely attempt to build a bridge into the other's world, through emphatic communication. Adam said it best, "She is bone of my bone and flesh of my flesh." What is the real meaning of two becoming one? This is far more than in the sexual area, but a unity of mind, will, and emotions; body, soul and spirit. When this happens, God's presence is manifest.

What about Gender dysphoria, and other gender fluid issues in the world today? Should young children be treated for these issues by the medical profession? What about the intersex continuum, where 2% of the world's population have distinctly unique DNA and chromosonal diversity? We can choose to hide our head in the sand while holding on to our "Binary" view of gender, or allow ourselves to be open to the facts about gender diversity in all of its complexity. This book addresses these contemporary issues.

In this book, I am endeavoring to communicate with two large communities, and our current political system. One of these is the Christian community and the Church at large. It is my desire to encourage more understanding, communication, bridge building and love. Obviously, there are parts of this community that have this going for them. The other community is the LGBTQ movement. I here recommend changes and improvements that will foster more understanding and receptivity, instead of "all out" conflict and political hostility. I trust my encouragements will be received with love by both communities.

Dani'El Garvin

CHAPTER ONE
THE BEGINNING OF GENDER

In the writings of Hebraic writings of creation in Genesis, Elohim said, *"Let us (Father, Son & Spirit) make man in our image, after our likeness. So Elohim created man (Ish) in His image. He created both male and female (Isha) and blessed them."*
<u>Note:</u> Eve was created here before her recreation from Adam's side. Eve preexisted within and apart of Adam, and both were created in God's image. At this point Adam was what we Natives call a 2-spirit person, and bi-gendered. God also was both "Abba" Father, and "El Shaddai" the breasted one and nursing mother.

Adam and Eve both were given the assignments to rule over the earth (Women have a leadership role), and they were to be fruitful and to multiply. Later in the creation writings, it describes the specifics of how they were formed. Yahovah (YHVH) formed man fron the dust of the ground (With the essence of Eve still within him), then YHVH blew the breath (Roark) into Adam's nostrils, and they became living souls.

Adam was then placed in the garden of paradise where there were 2-trees; the tree that gave life, and the tree which would bring death. Then YHVH saw that Adam needed a helper who would correspond to his essence. There was none in the animal kingdom. Then YHVH performs a surgical operation and places Adam in an anesthetized deep sleep. Next Yah cut out one of Adam's sides (Not ribs in Hebrew), and closed off the wound. Then YHVH recreated this part of Adam into a woman. In other words, a part of Adam was reformed into a female, which means "From male."

Because Eve originated from Adam's flesh and bones, their essence was the same, or *"One flesh"* equal in every way, yet with distinct roles and gifts. An example of this is, the Holy Spirit (Roark Ha Kodosh) is equally one with the Father, yet with distinct roles and gifts. The same is true with the Son, Yahshua Christ.

So, what are some implications of all this? Both male and female are of the same essence and being, of which the root source is the male. The male (Ish), flowed into becoming female (Isha), by the re-creative surgical hands of YHVH. Therefore, the original intent was that they were equals, who could correspond to the needs of the other, both with leadership status (*"They would rule;"* Genesis 1: 27,28).

It was only after the fall, that women were relegated to having a strong desire to submit to the man and have pain in child birth. This however was not the original creative plan. After Yahshua Christ bore all of their curse on the cross as the 2nd Adam, women now can access a return to their corresponding leadership status.

The original creative plan of YHVH was that both would rule and reign over creation, as they were transformed more and more into spirit-beings. As they ate from the tree of life, they had the potential of producing spiritual off-spring without pain. Before they sinned in rebellion, they were clothed with light, could access the supernatural realm, and could fellowship with angelic beings. In my book on amazon, "Paradise restored" I show how we can access what Adam and Eve missed out on, because of Christ paying the full price of the curse of the fall through His redemption.

We now can be clothed with light, from the light of the world our Savior. We can eat from the tree of life Yahshua, and be filled with the fruits of the Spirit. We now have direct access into the supernatural realm through our gate-keeper Yahshua Christ, who is our high priest. We can return again to our God ordained roles in creation. Therefore, we can operate now in corresponding gender unity, as originally intended.

CHAPTER TWO
THE GREAT DIVIDE

In the world today, there is a great divide between male and female. Huge walls have been erected, each side demanding precedence and superiority. Women who are still under the curse, are trying to overcome a male-dominated culture. It is rare to find equality and a consensus respectability which corresponds to God's original intent in creation.

Because of this, there is a dis-ownership of one's gender identity and creative roles today. No longer is there a sense of oneness and unity, as having the same essence and root source. Equality of leadership is a foreign concept. In the Church today, women are encouraged to be sweet, silent and submissive, and to walk in their husband's shadows. God forbid, if a woman aspired to be a pastor! Equality of salaries is non-existent. This was not YHVH's original intent. Both are to be equal and one, with different procreative roles regarding child bearing. These barriers of disunity need to come down! We need to see and appreciate each other's value and worth.

So, let's talk about how God's Son modeled love and compassion. These barriers were like huge mountains back in the time of Christ messiah. Women had the status of farm animals, and were among the "Untouchables." So, what did Yahovah think about this? Christ, who was the image of the invisible God, the exact likeness of His being, whose Hebrew name meant "Yahweh is salvation," gave great value and worth to women. He did not condemn the repentant woman caught in the act of adultery, who later became His follower. The woman at the well, a half-breed Samaritan enemy of the Jews, who on top of this, was much like a woman of ill repute. She had gone through 5-husbands, and was currently living with a man out of wedlock. Jews don't speak to women of this caliber, much less her own people. Yahshua Christ, who was God in the flesh, engaged her in conversation, after asking her for a drink of water. She became the first person that Jesus told that He was the messiah. He told her of the living water of His love that would satisfy her need for real love. She accepted and went back home, and was responsible for a major revival in her village. Church history verified that she later became an apostle in the ecclesial church of Christ.

Mary Magdeleine, was possessed with evil spirits, and through the loving hands of Christ was completely delivered and set free. She became a faithful follower and leader in the early Church. She was the first one that Yahshua revealed Himself to, after He rose from the dead...a woman, think of that! Christ gave great value and worth to this despised, subservient gender, to show us the divine intent for both genders from the beginning.

In my Native American culture, women had great value before the settlers came over. Clan mothers would appoint or remove the Chiefs, and were a key part of tribal councils, where they would give a generational perspective. They led in drum circles, and sweat lodge worship. When the Roman Catholic missionaries came over, they made women take a subservient role to walk behind their husbands in silent submission. They were told to be sweet, silent and submissive. Then these missionaries captured their children and placed them in abusive boarding schools, in the name of "Jesus," where many were abused and killed.

I personally believe that if women had more strong leadership roles in the affairs of nations, then there would be fewer wars.

Women care about what happens to future generations. Men tend to settle things by fighting it out in pride.

CHAPTER THREE
UNITING OF THE GENDERS

So, how can we bring about more unity between the genders? How can we build on each other's strengths? Is there a way to blend together as one (*"Bone of my bone, flesh of my flesh"*)? When one examines the female brain, usually the left side is dominant and somewhat larger than the right. The left dominant brain tends to be more verbal, detailed and factually and analytically oriented. Women generally do better in academia because of this. They possess great detail retention and tend to be perfectionist. Their verbal I.Q. score then, will be higher generally, than their performance I.Q.

Men on the other hand, are generally stronger in the performance right-brained functions. Of course there are exceptions on both sides. Most educational programs favor the verbal side of things. Men are stronger in performance right-brain functions. Men are great at doing things with their hands. However, in times of war and emergency, a man can access all parts of their brain. A woman on the other hand, has a protective barrier to prevent her being overwhelmed with emotions in times of crisis.

So, they both function best when the computers (Brains) of both genders are hooked in tandem. Conflict resolution can flow easy and fast because of this gender unity. When both work together at attacking the problem with possible solutions and strategies, instead of attacking each other, then resolution flows freely. Men are pre-programmed to quickly solve a problem, and most of the time fail to listen. They need to learn the valuable lesson that, quickly solving a problem doesn't solve anything, but accurately listening begins to solve the problem, when the woman feels she is understood. This is how women relate to other women, by listening and understanding. When one's words are valued, they feel valued, and their problems begin to fade away. Listening then, solves the problem, not attempting to solve the problem too quickly.

Try changing roles for a week to walk in each other's shoes. If your partner is a visual person, take the time to put your packets of words into picture form. If you are more visual, and your partner is verbal in communication, then translate the picture into packets of words in order to better communicate and understand. The same is true if you are more sensing/feeling, then translate the feelings into pictures or words. This is a way to build better bridges of understanding with each other. Try to really feel what the other feels. Again, listening with accuracy is the key to good communication.

CHAPTER FOUR
ADAPTING TO THE OTHER'S CULTURE

We are not all that different. Of course, there are the obvious procreative physical differences of "indoor" verses "outdoor" plumbing. Women also have larger breasts for nursing their offspring. Also, there are differences in hormonal chemistry. However, we both have many features in common: 5-fingers/toes, hands & feet, legs & arms/, hair & head and faces.

Society has attempted to mix the genders in a sort of unisex model, by placing both in a blender or melting pot, resulting in the tree of mixture (Good & evil) and confusion. However, it is true that there needs to be more communication and cultural understanding of different gender uniqueness's, in order to bring us closer as one. There needs to be a coming together and natural flow, respecting the context of each unique cultural role and naturally assigned fruitful destinies.

For instance, again in my Native American culture, the Roman Catholic church tried to change our culture into a western civilized culture through boarding school assimilation.

However, we have a different world view given by the Creator. The Church attempted to delete the Indian culture and to re-make us into westerners by abusive assimilation methods. Their Eugenic philosophy concluded that we were uncivilized savages without a soul. "Kill the Indian, and save the person" was their motto. Tribal children were captured in gun boats, placed in these abusive assimilation facilities, stripped of their names, given a number, their hair was cut, regalia burned, and were forbidden to speak their tribal language. No longer could they have a natural family. They were gifted small pox embedded blankets. Many were put into pedophile rooms for the pleasure of the priests, and some were even forcibly castrated, in the name of Jesus. This took place even in the late 60's.

However, our world view and culture would not blend, and it is being restored today. But much damage has been done. There are irreconcilable differences between our world view and the western world view, especially on how to care-take the earth and its resources. We do not value wealth-getting by raping the earth of it's resources and polluting the environment. There is some good history however, of people like William Bradford, Roger Williams, and Elliot, who through understanding and learning from our culture, built a bridge of understanding. This resulted in two generations of peaceful co-existence and "Praying Indians" who governed their own communities in New England. This was truly "A city on a hill" and modeled a godly way into deeper understanding. The movie "Dances with wolves is an example of this.

This bridge building and understanding, is what I suggest in removing gender barriers! This same concept can be applied to deeper understanding of the male and female cultures today, if we make the effort to understand each other's worlds.

CHAPTER FIVE
GENDER UNIQUENESSES

Now let's put a microscope on the various uniqueness's of gender identity. There are no two women alike, for instance. You have very sweet, feminine varieties, and you also have those who have strong masculine attributes. The same with men. You have the "Macho" John Wayne types, and you also have more sensitive, compassionate and nurturing men. Each of these varieties have value and worth, and needs special understanding. Then you have the intersex continuum. For instance, I am a Native American two-spirit, which is a gender fluid and highly celebrated identity in Native culture. We are a gift to the tribe. This is a spiritual rather than a sexual gifting. Two-spirit medicine warriors give wisdom to both genders, and live in both the natural realm and the supernatural realm.

Two percent of the world's population is intersex, as many as there are red heads in the world. There are 25-different DNA varieties within this continuum. You have some men with XX, and some women with XY, and tall athletic women who are XXXY. Then you have

Klinefelters and Hermaphrodite variations of having some physical features of both genders.

I recently saw a video of what looked like a normal woman, who said her body was natural except in place of her ovaries, she had testes. Years ago Doctors tried to surgically correct intersex anomalies, but today there is more acceptance for these differences. As you would imagine, understanding and communication is the key.

Even in the animal kingdom we see these differences. The male seahorse carries the eggs, and the clown fish changes from male to female, for instance. Other fish change gender in the opposite direction. Worms have both genders. There are many examples of this. Western culture has become fixated on the "Binary" view of gender. This view is rigid and lacks understanding of gender differences. Many politicians say they believe there is only two genders, and attempt to legislate this binary world view on to society.

One would then conclude that degeneration of the gene pool throughout history has damaged our originally created DNA. Another view, however, is that our Creator has created a multifaceted diversity in creation. Even Christ taught that some are naturally born eunuchs. I believe in the latter view.

Compassion, love and understanding is the key to building bridges with those we don't understand or even like. We then need to initiate communication with gender distinct individuals in our world today. Each are unique and different. Different doesn't mean bad. Allow people to be who they are, accept, embrace, and celebrate their differences. This is the way of love! Judgementalism increases the barriers to understanding. Everyone has value and worth.

CHAPTER SIX
THE TRANSGENDER PHENOMENON

I am not going to address the issues of gender sexual preferences, as this is an issue that each person must decide before their Creator, and to be accountable to Him. Not only that, it would take another whole book to adequately cover this subject. I have two such books on amazon.

Now, let's address the transgendered view of gender. One of my good friends wrote the definition of transgender for the dictionary, to simply be an overall encompassing term for gender dysphoria of all kinds. Most transgendered (Trans) people feel a complete disparity between who they feel they are on the inside, and their outward assigned gender at birth. They believe that their true identity is inscribed on their spirit. Their desire is to simply conform the outward persona, to be congruent with their inward sense of who they really are gender-wise. They often utilize dress, cross sex hormones, and some go through gender enhancement surgery. These surgical procedures can recreate for the male-to-female, female genitalia, and also many opt for breast augmentation. There are also surgical procedures for the female-to-male trans person. This helps to reinforce their new outward sense of who the feel like they really are intrinsically.

Some call this a "sex change", which is somewhat of a misnomer, as the trans person can really never become a cis-gendered (Natural born) man or woman. However many have successfully transitioned to complete living and working in their inward gender conviction, and some even have normal successful marriages and adopt children. I have a M-F trans friend who has been through successful transition and surgery, and has been happily married with grandchildren for over 50-years. She is a consultant for the VA and travels broadly to give lectures and update medical procedures. One time she accidentally went into the men's room and was quickly escorted out to the ladies room.

Trans people need a lot of love and understanding in our culture, as it is considered shameful for a man to exhibit feminine traits. The same is true for women with masculine traits. This demonstrates the power of staying within your birth assigned gender, because of the cultural fixation on the "Binary" which is, there are only two genders. Many transitioning trans people have been brutalized, beaten up, and killed for challenging the system. There is also a very high rate of suicide for this population. However progress is being made to foster communication and understanding. By the way, I am a psychotherapist with over 25-years experience, now in retirement.

Therefore, focusing on the inner person is the key, and not trying to change the outward transitional manifestations to conform to cultural pressure. Scripture states *"Man looks on the outward person, but God looks on the heart."*

Are the surgical options morally right? Is this an affront to God's natural creative order? Can God use Doctors to be apart of this re-creative process? It is interesting to me, when one studys circumcision in scripture, that God commands that a Rabbi perform a surgical procedure on a male baby, in order to confirm a covenant with the Creator. Think about this! "If an operation to alter genitalia was necessary to bring the male Jewish body into conformity with the Jewish soul, then God long ago acknowledged that medical intervention may be necessary for human beings to achieve their true identities." ("Through the door of life" by Joy Ladin)

I personally believe that God can use Doctors and the medical profession to work re-creative miracles in every area of our lives. From breast reconstruction in cancer patients, to knee replacements, separation of Siamese twins, to valve, organ, and heart repair. Thank God that the medical community serves us with the latest medical advancements!

One key area that is rarely focused on in transitional work, is the area of "self-rejection." There are many examples of trans people who feel that gender enhancement surgery is the "Magic bullet" to final self acceptance, only to realize afterwards that there were rejection issues that had nothing to do with gender, that needed to be attended to emotionally.

Many post-operative trans people, then desire more and more surgical procedures in order to magically change who they really are below the surface on the inside. Many of these end up in despair and depression, and some become suicidal. Therefore, It is my recommendation that adequate counseling prior to surgery is necessary, in order to deal with these rejection issues.

These issues are composed of early developmental deficits that need to be reconstructed in order to establish trust, unconditional love, and individuation. Also one needs to rebuild self-esteem and assertiveness, in order to blossom into their true identity. Self hatred and conditional love provide no foundation for a successful transition. You cannot escape from a rejected identity and try to establish a brand new "Fantasy identity" in another gender! This happens a lot and there are those who failed to find their new identity acceptable, then they want to reverse these surgical procedures, which are irreversible physically.

So, there is the need for a complete integration of body, soul, and spirit that needs to take place, so their newly adopted identity can fully blossom emotionally, as well as physically. This is why I am an advocate of the standards of care that were once required, but are now discarded by the medical and trans community. Also, these surgical procedures have become a source of financial wealth for the medical community. Therefore, we need to take stock and count the real cost, if self-rejection isn't properly treated to insure a higher percentage of success.

CHAPTER SEVEN
M-F TRANS (men) IN WOMEN'S SPORTS

Now on the subject of recently transitioning M-F trans people who enter into athletic competition with cis-gendered girls. Usually this is in the context of High School or College athletics. I have a definite opinion regarding this, which I communicated in a letter to the President. I feel that because of the obvious muscle mass advantage that these transitioning transgender individuals have, that they should be made to wait at least 3-years on hormone replacement, to equal out their muscle mass with that of other cis-gendered females. However, if they had puberty blockers prior to transitioning, they obviously would have similar muscle mass to their counterparts. Also, pre-surgical M-F trans men, should be restricted from cis-gendered girls dressing rooms.

This is an example where forced assimilation oversteps its boundaries through political activism. This hinders the ability to adjust to the complexities of transition in a way of mutual cooperation and understanding. Both the transgendered person and the normal school culture have to transition together, or it doesn't flow in love and unity.

There are many things in the LGBTQ political activist agenda that I do not agree with. The same disagreement is true with many of my trans friends who are elders in the movement. One cannot go from wanting acceptance, to demanding exclusivity without a political and cultural back lash. One area that I personally object to is, drag queens dressed in seductive clothing reading books to very young boys and girls. Also, some of the literature that is being forced into school libraries for children to read, is not appropriately written to build healthy bridges of understanding. That's all I have to say about that!

CHAPTER EIGHT
TREATMENT OF GENDER DYSPHORIA IN CHILDREN

This is a very controversial subject! This also has been a "Red hot" political issue which ends up being an "all-or-nothing" subject. On the conservative side, politicians run for office on the promise to do away with any possibility of this happening. Liberal politicians want it to continue for gender care. My question is, should this medical/psychological issue be politicized? This is another example of trying to legislate morality. Most politicians really have very little understanding of gender dysphoria.

This is one area that needs to be carefully vetted, with psychological counseling and medical supervision. Let's look carefully at the issues involved. Here we need to look at human development and abnormal psychology.

I like to summarize in a simple way, the three basic stages of development. The first stage I call the "Auto-erotic" stage. Here a young child goes through the phallic discovery of their genitals and sexual differences. But to me the main area is the important same-sex bonding that needs to occur. In the book "Iron John" he describes the cellular bonding that needs to take place between a boy and his father, and a girl and her mother. He states that only "Father water" can fill the boys' reservoir for identity. "Mother water cannot do it for young boys. Also, only "Mother water" can fill the young girls reservoir for female identity, not father water. That's not to say that the opposite sex parent cannot have a crucial role in their life. Therefore, same sex bonding and attachment of loving parents builds trust and basic identity.

Also, during this "Auto-erotic stage (Which covers many stages), there is the experimentation of opposite sex exploration and play, but doesn't usually last a long time. The next stage I call the "Homo-erotic" stage, where the blossoming child gets a strong sense of gender identity from same sex peer relationships. Girls tend to group-up with other girls and learn who they are within this context. They learn self esteem, how to assert themselves, and individuation, as they see themselves reflected off the mirror of their same sex peers. The same with boys. Through competitive sports, verbal and physical confrontations and the pecking order, they develop non-sexual love with best friends and the peer group identity. Later in life, they for the most part graduate to "Hetero-erotic" relationships, if stage one and two are intact.

It is difficult to define what the root issues are in childhood gender dysphoria. Yes, developmental deficits play a role, but some get stuck very early in life with an abnormal sense of their own gender identity, and reject their bodies and birth-sex classification.

I want to say at this point, I really favor waiting until later in life when they are emotionally mature enough to make gender reassignment decisions. The problem is that when puberty occurs, these changes to their physiology exacerbates gender dysphoria dramatically, and many become suicidal. For those parents of a child like this, they really need intense psychological and medical supervision, before deciding to use puberty blocking medication, along with cross sex hormones. This is because a large percentage eventually grow out of a gender change fixation. I firmly advise a standard of care vetting of children with gender dysphoria symptoms, because there are children who really need transitional help. Puberty blockers do give a few more years to figure things out, and if medically supervised, can be reversed. The same with cross-sex hormones.

I am not an expert in this area, but there have been successful outcomes in gender transition for children. One story, a conservative Christian mother who had a hatred for the LGBTQ movement, as it happened, she had a young son that constantly made appeals to her that he really was a girl! This mother took him for counseling and a full psychological assessment was made. Medical help was recommended. As she sought medical help, they diagnosed him with gender dysphoria. She tried her church and their healing ministry, with no effect. She exposed him to scripture and refused to acknowledge his struggle.

One day as she passed by his room, she heard him tearfully praying and asking God to take his life, if he couldn't be who he really was. His mother began to wake up to the seriousness of his struggle and asked the Doctor what she should do? He answered, if you were on a deserted island with him, would you allow him to live as the girl he is convinced that he is? She replied, "Yes I would." The Doctor replied, "The real issue, then is the social shame that you would have in your current life, that you would now have to face." The revelation of this truth made her change to prioritize her son's needs, and with the supportive help of these professionals, she gave her son permission to transition.

The results were dramatic, as she observed a now happy and blossoming young new daughter, that became fully functioning in all areas of her new life. She developed girl friends, and with the help of school counselors, easily transitioned into her female identity. Later she was placed on cross sex hormones and puberty blockers. She developed into a beautiful young girl. Later in life she could decide on gender enhancement surgical procedures to create female genitalia.

Observing these miraculous changes of God working through the medical profession, to see this recreation of her offspring, she went public and apologized for her hateful attitude toward the LGBTQ community. She asked for forgiveness for her lack of understanding and compassion. Now, all stories don't end up like this, which shows the need for responsible rules of treatment in order to adequately vet those with these issues. This is all I have to say about this!

CHAPTER NINE
THE PRE-EXISTENT WOMB

Many who are uncomfortable with their assigned birth gender, have a sense that before they were born in the womb, they had a pre-existent identity when they were still in the heart of their Creator. Yahovah said to the prophet Jeremiah, *"Before I formed you in the womb I knew you, and consecrated you."* This pre-womb place of being designed and consecrated, is where many trans people feel they were given their real spirit identities.

Also, while in the womb, everyone starts out being female. It's the father's dominant hormones changes things to become more male focused. The mother's hormonal balance also plays a part in the womb. Scientifically, there is evidence through MRI testing in the womb, that an infant may have developed male genitalia, but they can also have a female brain scan. This phenomenon is called "Brain sex." Then add to this the influence of maternal estrogen on the hypothalamus, which gives more of a female bias to the infant in the womb. Lastly, there is the influence of the HY-antigen, which also affects gender balance. Therefore, things aren't always as simple as the male/female rigid binary, but there is a lot of room for diversity of gender.

As I previously stated, when one takes a good look at nature and the animal kingdom, you also see this diversity of gender expressions in creation.

CHAPTER TEN
OUR GENDER IN HEAVEN

Then there is the issue of gender in the after-life. Yahshua Christ taught that in heaven we would all be like the angels with no procreation or sexual relationships. So, one would assume that we would all be asexual or neuter. Does this mean that our gender identities on earth would not be seen in heaven? Hmmm! Then you throw in the fact that we are to be the bride of Christ in heaven...Hmmm! Are we all to be female of some sort in order to be His bride? I personally think that this is talking about a close, intimate spiritual marriage, with the lover of our soul. Scripture says, *"Flesh and blood cannot inherit the kingdom of God."* We then, are talking about what is written in the Song of Solomon, a supernatural love and intimacy, with pure devotion and worship.

In my own life I feel I have broken through the gender barrier as a Native 2-spirit medicine warrior. I can identify with both the masculine and feminine persona in a gender-balanced way. My focus isn't on dress, sex, or even outward appearance. I don't require surgical procedures. I can easily carry myself in either world. Because of this I understand both worlds and can communicate easily and freely in either world. I frequently give wisdom to both male and female.

At powwows, I dance both the men's traditional warrior dances and the women's shawl dances. I am not bisexual, but more gender fluid. I have developed close friends in both gender worlds. I feel no sense of confusion and am not classified as transgendered. Because I have broken the gender barrier, many friends and family members have a hard time fitting me into their world view of gender identity. This is part of the price I pay for flying past the gender (Sound) barrier into a world largely unknown to our present culture.

However, my Native American culture celebrates me as a gift to tribal people as a holy medicine chief. In sweat lodge I have visions and dreams, and see into the supernatural world easily. To live in both the natural and supernatural realms is also part of being a Native 2-spirit. I give Native names to those within the sacred hoop. Ask any cultural Native what a 2-spirit is, and they will know. We are referred to as "Jewels." It is not an identity within the LGBTQ sexual spectrum, but is an ancient spiritual identity. Two spirits are not generally considered "Gay."

CHAPTER ELEVEN
GENDER IN OTHER CULTURES

Many nations have had multi-gendered classifications in place for years. Can we not see the beauty in gender diversity? The Asian nation that I did mission work in, has several gender classifications. Many cultures celebrate a 2-spirit type of individual to perform spiritual ceremonies. The Jewish culture also makes room for gender diversity.

For instance, in the Hindu culture, you have a gender classification called "Hijra" which flows out of the intersex continuum. This bi-gendered person is involved in sacred spirituality and religious roles. They often preside over weddings and new births to give their blessing.

In South Sulawesi, Indonesia, you find bi-gendered individuals known as "Calalai"or "Calabai" or "Bissu" who have initial female beginnings, but who present as males and take on men's leadership roles. They dress as males, wear sacred daggers, and spiritually bridge both the natural and supernatural worlds. They oversee marriages and other sacred ceremonies.

In Mexico, originally part of the Zapotec people in the Oaxaca state, you have individuals known as the "Muxe." These began as male but take on a distinct female domestic role in the home. They are very honored in that culture.

In Madagascar, you find the "Sekrata" individuals with male characteristics, but develop female characteristics and behavior from early childhood. They are raised as female and perform spiritual ceremonies.

In the Philippines, you find the "Bakia" with the same bi-gendered gifting of balancing both the masculine and feminine, and are considered leaders of their communities.

As previously mentioned, in the Native American culture tribal people consider it a gift to the tribe if someone is born a two-spirit medicine warrior. This is an ancient gender fluid identity that is within the intersex continuum. As previously mentioned the two-spirit has the balance of both masculine and feminine identities, and can live, work, and give wisdom to both genders. A two-spirit also is a spiritual individual who lives in both the natural and supernatural worlds. The focus of the two-spirit is not sexuality. Against a popular viewpoint, the two-spirit is not a "gay" person. It is my conviction that the two-spirit identity should never be incorporated into the more recent evolution of the LGBTQ spectrum.

As I mentioned, the main focus of the two-spirit is a life in the spirit, and their leadership in sacred ceremonies. In sweat lodge, they have visions and dreams, and often give out native names.

Holy living is expected of the Native two-spirit in tribal settings. We are gender fluid respected members of the tribe. We are a more ancient gender identity than is expressed in the more recent LGBTQ movement. We do not want to have our traditional identity changed or altered in any way. The early settlers tried to give us a distorted name called "Berdache" which tried to incorporate us into their Greek/Roman concept of youth, who were castrated for the sexual pleasure of heterosexual men. We don't want to be anything other than who we are.

As a Native American 2-spirit I've been experiencing the abundant life and am extremely happy. I walk in personal holiness with the Creator and am very much in love with Him. Remember, He is both "Abba" father, and "El

Shaddai" the breasted nursing mother. I do not sexualize this spiritual identity. Therefore, I can experience both the feminine and masculine worlds, and also the natural and the supernatural realms. I accept and honor this gifting.

CHAPTER TWELVE
MORALITY AND GENDER

So, what is the morality of gender identity? Does not God look at the heart as being the central focus? Is it not part of salvation to transform the whole person? Does not the Father and the Son want us to live an abundant life, one full and meaningful? Are gender identity issues too complex for God to bring His love into, and to help the struggling soul?

In Jeremiah 18, it describes a creator potter fashioning a pot on the wheel. The first pot was spoiled, so he refashioned another pot out of the same clay as the first one. Then God concludes that He can deal with us in like manner as this. I ask the question here, "Cannot the Creator do re-creative miracles?" Saving, transforming, bringing new life, and change are a part of saving every part of us. In 1 Thessalonians 5: 23 it states, *"Now may the God of peace sanctify (Save) you completely, may your whole body, soul and spirit be preserved complete at His coming."* In other words, bringing salvation in every part of who we are, is a part of the sanctification process. He desires that we be complete and whole in every facet of our being.

No struggle is impossible for Him to bring change to, and to love us through to completion.

Who can really say what is a sin in God's eyes? David was vindicated even though he ate the shew bread which was against the law. Christ taught on this, that mercy is better than sacrifice. In other words, the law of love is higher than the letter of the law. Hosea was told by God to marry a prostitute to show Israel their unfaithfulness. Rehab lied about the spies being with her, she was a harlot, yet somehow her future generations produced the lineage of Christ the messiah. Ruth was a gentile pagan temple prostitute, but ended up producing the lineage of David. Samson, was led by the Holy Spirit to marry a Philistine (Non-Jewish) woman, so that her people would be destroyed by him. There are many places in scripture where this occurs. Therefore mercy and love, not sacrifice seems to be congruent with God's nature.

Today many conservative politicians are lining up behind the "Binary" view of gender identity. "There are only two genders!" they proclaim. This obviously is not scientifically or medically true. Then they harp on the "Bathroom issue," with the assumption that transitioning trans people are sexual deviates who only want to spy out cis-gendered people for sexual addictive pleasure. I have never encountered a trans person with these issues. Those in the heterosexual lifestyle are more prone to this behavior. Trans people simply just want to use the rest room to relieve themselves like everyone else.

Imagine with me that a M-F transitioning trans person is wearing a decent dress with appropriate hair and make-up, going into the men's room. They would either be escorted to the women's room, or they would be beat up. Thankfully, multigendered rest rooms are becoming the norm, as they are on airplanes. But this issue gets a lot of votes politically. The biggest issue in politics today is the issue of young transitioning M-F trans in women's sports. I have already given you what I feel about this.

The general public doesn't realize that there are two groups within the LGBTQ community. The first are the more militant political activist, who I feel have gone beyond wanting equality to now demanding exclusivity. This change of focus has created a backlash in the conservative political world.

I have been a part of an elder's movement within the LGBTQ community, many of which do not agree with the focus of the militant political activist on many of their issues and demands. I do not consider myself to be in any way gay. Yet, as a Native 2-spirit I am given access into their world and culture. When in their community, I hug, love and share Yahshua Christ with these my friends. Once Yahshua gets inside a person, He makes any necessary changes from the inside out. I believe we all, especially the church, need to make room at the table of love for everyone! (My book "Room at the Table" on amazon) Believe it or not, there are those within the heterosexual lifestyle, that also have struggles and need to be loved.

My view on politicizing gender issues is, to avoid being involved with legislating morality, because America is not a theocracy like Iran, for instance. Therefore, moral issues belong at the feet of our Creator on a personal and individual basis. Aho!

CHAPTER FOURTEEN
CONCLUSION OF THE MATTER

So, I hope that you now can see that it is possible to break through the gender barrier. It starts with opening up yourself to the diversity of God's creation, both in the natural, and animal world, and among physical human life all around us.

Yahovah is a many faceted God, with 365 names describing all of His uniqueness's. One day we will learn more about all of His diverse facets in eternity. Would not then His creation have many diverse facets, that when celebrated, project the light's brilliance like a multifaceted diamond ring?

I appeal to conservative Christians, that you need to reconsider your "All-or-nothing" approach to gender issues. Hatred is not Biblical or spiritual! Love and compassion wins the day! Bridge building is taught in John 3:16. God loved us before we even loved Him. Therefore, self-righteous finger pointing, critical language, and constructing walls is not Christian! Any one of us have the potential of struggling with any issue that life throws at us. We need to remove the log of critical hatred in our eyes and begin to see through the lenses of God's love.

Now to the LGBTQ community, this book is written to expose areas that could bring negative reactions and responses by way of backlash from both conservative Christians, and politicians and educators. The LGBTQ community needs to get its act together in order to preserve communication and understanding, and to not start a war which will bring separation and violence. Somehow there needs to be a coordination between LGBTQ people in everyday life, and the fiery LGBTQ political activists, who seem to only represent their own agenda of exclusivity. Overkill by forced exposure to inappropriate literature, and the inordinate pressure to unfairly force M-F trans youth into athletic competitions with cis-gendered girls sports, without a proper transitional protocol, are examples of this.

Also, the LGBTQ community needs to communicate the difference between positive and negative pride, that it is not about narcissistic pride. I also feel that the rules of treatment need to be reinstated for proper vetting of those with gender dysphoria, to prevent disasters of suicide and self-mutilation.

We need to return to standards of care to bring a more positive outcome. Also, there is the need of training in the area of safety, so that rape and murder doesn't occur. We need to work with those who haven't integrated career planning, to take care of their financial provision, instead of needing to prostitute themselves. Also, what's with all the new gender labels??

Elders need to be raised up to bring sanity by writing basic labels that give overall identification to gender issues. Let's not give up on the goals of acceptance and being celebrated for personal choices made before our higher power.

Communication and understanding opens the door to breakthrough. I suggest that you give it a go, and start by focused listening in order to have empathy, feel what the other person feels, and to put yourself in their shoes. Try not to judge or limit the possibilities for growth and change. Remove rigidity and begin to embrace flexibility as you begin to have a more open mind and spirit of love! Aho!

"Stop assuming an outward expression that does not come from within you, and is not representative of what you are in your inner

being, but is patterned after this age; but change your outward expression to one that comes from within and is representative of your inner being by the renewing of your mind, resulting in your putting to the test what is the will of God, the good and well-pleasing and complete will, and having found that it meets specifications, place your approval on it."
(Wuest translation from the Greek)
Romans 12: 2

ABOUT THE AUTHOR

Dani'El Garvin is a Writer, Poet, Author, Missionary, Native American, Indigenous Counselor, and Conference Speaker.

Contact:
E-Mail at agapedan1@aol.com

For All Of Dani'El Garvin's Books, You May Go Directly To Dani'El's Amazon Author Page At https://bit.ly/Daniel-Garvin